Praise for Healthy Money

Out of the depth and breadth of their faith and experience, the Picardo's have developed a resource to help any Christian person or family to mature from fear and anxiety about dealing with money to faithfulness and generosity.

Gregory Vaughn Palmer, Bishop, West Ohio Conference,
The United Methodist Church

I pay attention to any good resource about money, knowing money has such a huge hold on our people. I'm excited about this one by Roz and Callie. They've put a lot of *gold* into one book. This will immediately go into my library of recommendations.

Ron Edmondson, pastor, author, consultant,
RonEdmondson.com

Roz and Callie care deeply about helping God's people become spiritually discipled into faith-filled stewardship of their financial resources—and their passion clearly shines through each page of this book. What a useful tool to help readers become self-aware of their relationship with money and receive motivation to seek financial health!

Rev. Sue Nilson Kibbey, Director, Bishop Bruce Ough Innovation
Center, United Theological Seminary, Dayton, Ohio

This is a wise and practical 30-day devotional prayer guide which helps us understand how we developed our attitudes towards finances and gives us relevant Scriptural wisdom as we seek to grow in our understanding of God's desire to love and bless us in every area of life. *Healthy Money* helps God heal us from unhealthy attitudes and actions regarding our finances. I highly recommend it

Dr. Kent Millard, President, United Theological Seminary,
Dayton, Ohio

The Picardos have written a practical book rooted in scripture and lived experience. The daily readings helped me reflect on my approach to finances and challenged me to grow. I can't wait to read it again with my wife and see how it can help us in our faith and finances.

Luke Edwards, author of *Becoming Church: A Trail Guide for Starting Fresh Expressions*, Associate Director of Church Development, Fresh Expressions and Innovation, Western NC Conference, The United Methodist Church

An incredibly practical resource for financial health. Jesus came to set the oppressed free! One of the greatest oppressive forces in American culture today for the average family is the burden of debt. Debt fueled by the luring idols of materialism. Roz and Callie's 30-day devotional journey will keep you on a path of financial wholeness.

Mike Slaughter, Founder & Chief Strategist, Passionate Churches, LLC

Healthy Money is a wonderful and easy to read resource on what is often a very difficult subject—yet it is so important for healthy marriages and healthy spiritual lives. Highly recommended!

Angela Correll, author of *Restored in Tuscany: A True Story of Facing Loss, Finding Beauty and Living Forward in Hope*

Roz and Callie Picardo have devoted their lives to helping people experience liberation through God's love. *Healthy Money* is a helpful tool towards wholeness.

Rev. Laura Baber, Spiritual Director and retired United Methodist Deacon

Money stuff can be so stressful. It can weigh you down and hold you back. This book offers a better way through a simple, daily journey with God. This is the best resource I have seen for a practical, powerful path to find freedom with your finances!

Jacob Armstrong, Pastor, Providence Church, Mt. Juliet TN, author of *Breaking Open*

One of the prayers I regularly pray is "God, show me me." It's an acknowledgement of my propensity to self-deceive. Roz and Callie have given the Body of Christ a great gift in *Healthy Money* to carefully heighten our self-awareness around how we each uniquely manage or mismanage money and the stuff money buys. This tool assists the Holy Spirit in helping us take our next step toward wellness in our finances.

Rev. Dr. Jorge Acevedo, leadership coach, writer, speaker, retired pastor

This book, rich with practical advice and insightful wisdom, is an invaluable companion for anyone seeking a transformative approach to financial health. Engaging and thought-provoking, this resource is one you'll likely return to yearly to deepen the lessons learned during the first 30 days. I strongly recommend you pick up this book and buy copies for those in your life struggling with financial challenges.

Jason Moore, Midnight Oil Production, author, speaker, consultant

Many churches today are challenged financially. This resource from Callie and Roz Picardo places focus where it needs to be, on individuals and groups growing on their generosity walk with God. Make the investment. Spend thirty days on this journey and see what God can do in your life and church.

Ken Willard, Director of Congregational Vitality West Virginia, The United Methodist Church, author, professionally certified coach

Healthy Money is a timely and helpful guide to exploring the connection between faith and money. Readers are invited to examine how their relationships with money were shaped and how God is inviting them into a new, more God-centered, relationship with money.

Kristine Miller, CFRE, ACC, Partner and Executive Vice President, Horizons Stewardship

Healthy Money: A 30-Day Journey toward Spiritual, Emotional, and Financial Freedom is different from many of the other finance-based resources. This book walks you through a daily journey over a 30-day period that allows the reader to reflect on progress and small wins to maintain engagement and encouragement. This book is a great resource for anyone who is looking to reduce debt or sharpen stewardship skills. The Picardos offer an invaluable tool for the toolbox, grounded in scripture.

Brad Aycock, Director of Fresh Starts & New Beginnings,
West Ohio Conference of The United Methodist Church

Callie and Roz draw us deeper into our collective story of faith as we seek to weave one of the most tangible acts of faith into our daily lives. This resource nudges us towards aligning our money habits with our spiritual habits - in the hopes that they will become a natural part of our everyday faith. This book is deeply spiritual and yet as practical as ever!

Rev. Rob Hutchinson, Director of Church Development,
Western NC Conference, The United Methodist Church

Healthy
Money

ROSARIO PICARDO
CALLIE PICARDO

A 30-Day Journey toward Spiritual, Emotional, and Financial Freedom

Healthy Money

invite
PRESS

Plano, Texas

Healthy Money
A 30-Day Journey toward Spiritual, Emotional, and Financial Freedom

Copyright 2024 by Rosario Picardo and Callie Picardo

This book is printed on acid-free, elemental chlorine-free paper.

ISBN Paperback: 978-1-953495-99-0; eBook 978-1-963265-00-2

All scripture quotations unless noted otherwise are taken from THE HOLY BIBLE, NEW INTERNATIONAL VERSION®, NIV® Copyright© 1973, 1978, 1984, 2011 by Biblica, Inc.™ Used by permission of Zondervan. All rights reserved worldwide.

Scripture quotations marked NRSV are taken from the New Revised Standard Version of the Bible, copyright 1989, Division of Christian Education of the National Council of the Churches of Christ in the United States of America. Used by permission. All rights reserved.

24 25 26 27 28 29 30 31 32 33—10 9 8 7 6 5 4 3 2 1
MANUFACTURED in the UNITED STATES of AMERICA

To our three little women of God:
Lily

Gabriella

Hannah

May you always know God's love,
and trust God with your whole heart.

Use the QR code below for a **FREE HEALTHY MONEY ASSESSMENT** quiz to help you discover your financial mindset, with results ranking your five mindsets in order from greatest to least.

Contents

Contents

Introduction

What is your money mindset? Does it help you or hold you back with certain financial goals? How was money handled growing up in your home and what financial experiences have you had in your adult years?

Many people know the right things to do with finances. They know they need to live within a budget, prioritize giving and saving, and avoid debt, but they still don't do it. It's not knowledge that is the problem. It is getting to what is underneath the surface. Often finances are only the tip of the iceberg. They are what is visible, but most of the iceberg is underneath the surface unseen. In order to impact your finances, you have to get to the mindset underneath the financial symptoms to find true wholeness and healing. It is a journey, but like any good journey, it often starts with a step.

You are invited on a five-week journey. This journey will not only include you and this book but God guiding you beneath the surface for greater awareness, healing, and courage to move forward faithfully with your finances toward your God-given dreams and goals.

Each day will be grounded in scripture because there are 2,350 verses on money and possessions in the Bible.[1] There is power in knowing what God's Word says about money.

---

1.   See *2350 Verses on Money and Possessions*, (Orlando: Compass, 2022), https://compass1.org/wp-content/uploads/2022/02/2350-Verses-Catalog.pdf.

Each day will also include a devotional thought followed by discussion questions to prompt your conversation with God around your own finances. You can go through these questions on your own or share what you are learning with a spouse, a close friend, a spiritual mentor, or a trusted small group. These can also guide you if you are going through premarital counseling with a future spouse.

Finally, each day ends with prayer. We have seen God move in mighty ways in response to prayer, but with finances, prayer is most often used only in times of crisis. What might God want to do if you pray daily for your finances for five weeks?

The journey will move through five sections of six days each. If you are meeting weekly with someone or a small group, you can do the journey over five weeks, with the seventh day being the meeting day. You can also continue straight through over thirty days, but after each six days there will be a space to pause and reflect on what you've learned, where you've been on the journey, and where you are going.

The journey starts with identifying your money mindset. Then it moves to looking back. If we don't know where we've been, it's hard to know where we are going. After looking at childhood money memories and how your family of origin handled finance, we will look at what you've come through financially as an adult, or from the time you've been making your own financial decisions. In the fourth section of the journey, we will move intentionally toward health, replacing lies with the truth, strongholds with spiritual disciplines, and bringing areas that need healing to the Lord. Then, it's time to dream, to vision with God for the future. As this five-week journey comes to an end, where is God inviting you to go next?

At the end of these five weeks, our hope is that you will have greater awareness of what is behind your everyday financial decisions and be armed with prayers and tools to use when you notice old patterns impacting your life today. As you heal and grow in areas of your finances, we pray it grows you in your journey with the Lord as a faithful disciple of Jesus Christ in all areas of your life.

....

Lord, we pray that this beloved child of God reading this book would come to know you in deeper ways on this five-week journey. May this person experience your freedom, your healing, your deliverance from lies and bondage, your goodness, your faithfulness, your love, and your grace. May your Holy Spirit be this journey's guide, and may you move at your perfect pace of grace. Your will, your way, Lord. In Jesus' name, amen.

Money Mindsets

Day 1: Money Mindset

Scripture: Psalm 139:1-4, 13-16

> You have searched me, LORD,
> and you know me.
> You know when I sit and when I rise;
> you perceive my thoughts from afar.
> You discern my going out and my lying down;
> you are familiar with all my ways.
> Before a word is on my tongue
> you, LORD, know it completely . . .
> For you created my inmost being;
> you knit me together in my mother's womb.
> I praise you because I am fearfully and wonderfully made;
> your works are wonderful,
> I know that full well.
> My frame was not hidden from you
> when I was made in the secret place,
> when I was woven together in the depths of the earth.
> Your eyes saw my unformed body;
> all the days ordained for me were written in your book
> before one of them came to be.

It has been said that to really know ourselves, we must know *who* we are and *whose* we are. As Christians, we believe we are created by God and God does not make mistakes. God formed you in your mother's womb, and nothing is hidden from God. God knows you inside and out better than you could know yourself. Before a word is even formed on your tongue, God knows it. God knows us fully and loves us unconditionally. So, we can do whatever we want, right?

As our friend Pastor Wayne Botkin likes to say, "God loves you exactly as you are, and he loves you enough not to leave you there."

Whether you believe you are who you are by nature or nurture or a combination of both, God is at work in us by the power of the Holy Spirit to help us grow in wholeness and in holiness.

What does any of this have to do with finances, you might ask? We all have certain wirings, who we are because of our personality and life experiences. That impacts the way we relate to money and possessions. It makes budgeting easier for some and harder for others. It helps some people be generous and others save every penny. All of us have strengths and areas in which we need to grow as we mature in our faith and look a little more like Jesus today than we did yesterday.

Reflection Questions

As you prepare for this journey, what are some areas of strength and potential areas of growth as you manage your finances and possessions?

....

God, I believe I am fearfully and wonderfully made. Thank you for creating me, knowing me, and loving me. I want to grow a little more like Jesus each day of my life. Amen.

Sanctification is possessing the mind of Christ.
—John G. Lake

Day 2: Security Mindset

Scripture: Matthew 6:25-34

"Therefore I tell you, do not worry about your life, what you will eat or drink; or about your body, what you will wear. Is not life more than food, and the body more than clothes? Look at the birds of the air; they do not sow or reap or store away in barns, and yet your heavenly Father feeds them. Are you not much more valuable than they? Can any one of you by worrying add a single hour to your life?

"And why do you worry about clothes? See how the flowers of the field grow. They do not labor or spin. Yet I tell you that not even Solomon in all his splendor was dressed like one of these. If that is how God clothes the grass of the field, which is here today and tomorrow is thrown into the fire, will he not much more clothe you—you of little faith? So do not worry, saying, 'What shall we eat?' or 'What shall we drink?' or 'What shall we wear?' For the pagans run after all these things, and your heavenly Father knows that you need them. But seek first his kingdom and his righteousness, and all these things will be given to you as well. Therefore do not worry about tomorrow, for tomorrow will worry about itself. Each day has enough trouble of its own."

Where does your sense of security come from? God or money? That is the temptation for those with a security mindset. Often, it comes from an experience of not having enough, from declaring bankruptcy, from the anxiety of not knowing how needs would be met. Other times it comes from hearing of others or knowing people who have suddenly lost everything. It can also simply be that a strong sense of the need to save was instilled in you at an early age.

Those with a security mindset tend to be great savers. They know the benefits of having an emergency fund and saving for the future. They are patient with purchases and can handle delayed gratification. They understand that money is finite, so they prioritize long-term goals. These individuals are generally good with a budget. They budget conservatively and spend less than they earn.

The challenge is that a security mindset can easily become a scarcity mindset, believing there is never enough, which can lead to fear, anxiety, the idol of control, or perfectionism. It can also lead to anger if someone with a security mindset shares finances with those who tend to spend or give more—for example, those with a collector, carpe diem, or benevolence mindset.

Beneath it all is a question of where security ultimately comes from. Does it come from God or money?

Characteristics of a healthy security mindset:

- Spending within a budget
- Saving for the future and bigger purchases
- Taking modest risks
- Choosing to spend money on what matters most

Characteristics of an unhealthy security mindset:

- Hoarding
- Unwillingness to give or spend
- Obsessively checking investments
- Fear of disaster
- Anxiety over spending, even on budgeted items

Reflection Questions

On a scale of 1 to 10 (10 being the highest), how much do you think a security mindset describes you? Which of these characteristics do you notice in your own life?

How have you been impacted by others with a security mindset (family, friends, work colleagues, etc.)?

....

God, I want to trust you more. Please increase my faith and help me look to you as my ultimate source of security. Thank you for your promise to be with me always, to help me, and to keep me. Amen.

Never be afraid to trust an unknown future to a known God.
—Corrie ten Boom

Day 3: Collector Mindset

Scripture: 1 Kings 7:51

When all the work King Solomon had done for the temple of the LORD was finished, he brought in the things his father David had dedicated—the silver and gold and the furnishings—and he placed them in the treasuries of the LORD's temple.

Scripture: Matthew 13:45-46

"Again, the kingdom of heaven is like a merchant looking for fine pearls. When he found one of great value, he went away and sold everything he had and bought it."

With each of these mindsets, the heart is more important than the possessions, but when possessions start to take possession of your heart, then there is a problem. The collector appreciates high-quality items and cares for them. This might be antiques, cars, art, memorabilia, or things of value or at least perceived value in the eye of the beholder. As the old adage goes, "One man's junk is another man's treasure!" The temptation is to fall into materialism, greed, and finding identity in things. Hence, it is the heart that matters most.

Consider King Solomon, who built the temple of the Lord. He cared for every detail. He used the resources his father, King David, had collected and dedicated them to the Lord. He then filled the treasuries of the Lord's temple.

Many have continued, like King Solomon, to create beautiful spaces of worship and incredible cathedrals. Some have done this for their own egos, but others have truly done it for the love of the Lord and desire to lead others to worship God as King David did.

Just as collections have been used in worship of the Lord, they have been used as excuses to accumulate more. Stuff can become your source of worth or status. Greed, pride, envy, and comparison can creep in and take over.

There is a treasure worth far more than any earthly possession. Jesus tells a parable in Matthew 13:45-46 of the kingdom as a pearl of great price. He said, "Again, the kingdom of heaven is like a merchant looking for fine pearls. When he found one of great value, he went away and sold everything he had and bought it." That collector mindset when applied to faith leads us to sell all we have for a treasure worth more than any earthly thing.

At the same time, collections can be used to build relationships and share about your love for the Lord. A nice home can be used for hospitality. Relationships with those who have a similar affinity, say, for collecting antique cars, can create an open door for sharing about the good news of Jesus Christ, the pearl of great price. Which do you value more: the created thing or the Creator?
Characteristics of a healthy collector mindset:

- Buying things of value and quality and using them for the kingdom
- Building relationships with others of similar interest to share the good news
- Enjoying what they have, but not allowing those things to determine self-worth

Characteristics of an unhealthy collector mindset:

- Determing worth by what they have or do not have
- Constant comparison to others
- Focus on things over relationships

Reflection Questions:

On a scale of 1 to 10 (10 being the highest), how much do you think a collector mindset describes you? Which of these characteristics do you notice in your own life?

How have you been impacted by others with a collector mindset (family, friends, work colleagues, etc.)?

....

God, I want all that I have to be used for your glory. I offer to you my home, my vehicles, my money, and all of my possessions. Use those things to help others come to know you, "the pearl of great price." Amen.

The best and most beautiful things in the world cannot be seen or even touched. They must be felt with the heart.
—Helen Keller

Day 4: Benevolence Mindset

Scripture: Acts 20:35

"It is more blessed to give than to receive."

What could be more godly than giving? God is a generous God, who so loved the world that he gave his only Son for our salvation (John 3:16). All Christians are called to give, to invest in God's Kingdom and to care for the poor. Yet, giving is also a gift of the Spirit that some Christians have. Perhaps that's you if you have a benevolence mindset.

Those with a benevolence mindset love to give and help others. They may focus that giving on their friends and family or on their church and nonprofits or even strangers. Wherever they focus, these folks love to give generously. Gift giving is their love language. They enjoy finding the perfect gift to bring another person joy.

But is all giving good? Some give to the extreme of an unhealthy self-neglect. This is different from those who have taken a spiritual vow of poverty. This is a perspective that tends toward self-hatred—"I'm not worthy of anything good." It can also tend toward guilt—"I'm a bad person/Christian if I have anything nice." What if God wants to bless you with good gifts that are just for you, in addition to using you to bless others?

In *Sensible Shoes: A Story about the Spiritual Journey*, author Sharon Garlough Brown develops a character named Hannah who is always caring for others to the point of burnout, and as she moves toward healing, she hears the Lord speak to her heart: "The flowers are for you, Hannah. The flowers are for you."[1] She had spent her life giving everything she received from God to others when the

---

1. Sharon Garlough Brown, *Sensible Shoes: A Story about the Spiritual Journey* (Downers Grove, IL: IVP Books, 2013), 252.

Lord wanted to bless her as well. As you bless others, are you able also to receive a gift from the Lord just for you, or a gift from a friend or family member for you to enjoy?

Some with the benevolence mindset can also tend toward codependency. They go to the extreme in caring for those around them to the point that they are enabling others. Even though they want to help, at this point, their generosity is doing harm.

If guilt or people pleasing are motivating their giving, there is an opportunity for spiritual growth. If a sense that the one giving is a "savior" has entered the heart, there is a need for repentance. Jesus is the true Savior.

God's invitation is for us to partner in what the Lord is already doing in the world and to let the Holy Spirit lead us in our giving. Take some time to pray; thank God for the incredible gifts God has given you to enjoy; ask the Holy Spirit to show you any areas for growth or repentance, and then invite the Holy Spirit to lead you in your giving.

In health, those with a benevolence mindset use their generosity to build up God's Kingdom and encourage others as generosity champions. They take care of the needs of their family, but they live simply in order to give generously.

Characteristics of a healthy benevolence mindset:

- Giving generously to build up God's Kingdom
- Coming up with creative ways to bless others
- Giving motivated by compassion and a love for God and others

Characteristics of an unhealthy benevolence mindset:

- Giving motivated by people-pleasing, codependency, or a "savior complex"
- An inability to enjoy anything they have without a deep sense of guilt or shame for having anything nice

Reflection Questions

On a scale of 1 to 10 (10 being the highest) how much do you think a benevolence mindset describes you? Which of these characteristics do you notice in your own life?

How have you been impacted by others with a benevolence mindset (family, friends, work colleagues, etc.)?

....

God, thank you for the ultimate gift of your only Son for my salvation! Thank you for all you have given me. Holy Spirit, please lead me in my generosity. Show me what to enjoy and where I can be a blessing to others. May my giving always be for your glory and not my own. Amen.

No one has ever become poor by giving.
—Anne Frank

Day 5: Carpe Diem Mindset

Scripture: James 4:13-15

> Now listen, you who say, "Today or tomorrow we will go to this or that city, spend a year there, carry on business and make money." Why, you do not even know what will happen tomorrow. What is your life? You are a mist that appears for a little while and then vanishes. Instead, you ought to say, "If it is the Lord's will, we will live and do this or that."

In the movie *Dead Poets Society*, English teacher John Keating (played by Robin Williams) encourages his students, "Carpe diem. Seize the day, boys. Make your lives extraordinary."[1] This is the motto of those with the Carpe Diem Mindset. Those who live by carpe diem (Latin for "seize the day") know that tomorrow is not promised, so they make the most of today.

A mother of young children overcame cancer, and she and her husband decided to prioritize making memories and enjoying life *now* because cancer was a wakeup call that reminded them of the brevity of life. Rather than saving every penny for the future they may or may not share together, they began intentionally investing in making memories with their family today through special family trips and everyday moments.

Those with a carpe diem mindset are good at celebrating life. They value experiences over stuff and want to create special memories, often with those they love.

The temptation is to spend constantly and never to save. Delayed gratification and working toward long-term goals can be a

---

1. Peter Weir, "Dead Poets Society," Touchstone Pictures Silver Screen Partners IV, 1989.

challenge. In health, the person with a carpe diem mindset has learned the balance of prioritizing needs, saving regularly, but also enjoying special moments and experiences with God and others, and using those moments to build relationships to share God's love.

Characteristics of a healthy carpe diem mindset:

- Living for God today and sharing the love and gospel of Jesus Christ with others now
- Building relationships through special moments and memories with people who matter
- Helping others experience joy in this life and celebrate

Characteristics of an unhealthy carpe diem mindset:

- Spending constantly and never saving
- Addiction to thrills and new experiences that become the focus
- Impatience and an unwillingness to wait or work toward long-term goals
- Self-focused on what feels good rather than what is God-focused

Reflection Questions

On a scale of 1 to 10 (10 being the highest) how much do you think a carpe diem mindset describes you? Which of these characteristics do you notice in your own life?

How have you been impacted by others with a carpe diem mindset (family, friends, work colleagues, etc.)?

....

God, thank you for the gift of today. Help me to live for you each and every day. Show me when to save and when to spend and when to give. Help me prioritize loving you and others with my finances and my entire life. Amen.

Don't count the days, make the days count.
—Muhammad Ali

Day 6: Laissez-Faire Mindset

Scripture: Philippians 4:11-12

> I have learned to be content whatever the circumstances.
> I know what it is to be in need, and I know what it is to
> have plenty. I have learned the secret of being content
> in any and every situation, whether well fed or hungry,
> whether living in plenty or in want.

L*aissez-faire* is a French phrase that means "allow to do." Those with a laissez-faire mindset tend to go with the flow and be relaxed. With finances, they aren't overly focused on money or possessions. It is honestly a hard mindset to cultivate in the United States of America or other countries where advertisements abound, designed to make you discontent so that you will buy things whether you truly need them or not. In order to buy them, you have to have money.

Yet, Jesus, in the Sermon on the Mount teaches, "Therefore I tell you, do not worry about your life, what you will eat or drink; or about your body, what you will wear. Is not life more than food, and the body more than clothes? . . . Your heavenly Father knows that you need them" (Matthew 6:25, 32). God invites us to trust him with our needs and not to obsess over food and clothing, let alone a new car or the latest phone or gadget. The apostle Paul echoes a similar sentiment in his letter to the Philippians, saying, "I have learned to be content whatever the circumstances. I know what it is to be in need, and I know what it is to have plenty. I have learned the secret of being content in any and every situation, whether well fed or hungry, whether living in plenty or in want" (Philippians 4:11-12). There is power in contentment, and those with a healthy laissez-faire mindset have learned this secret power. They enjoy a peace when it comes to their finances and live simply, focusing on the more important things in life: loving God and others. They seek God first, and trust God.

Just as with all of the mindsets, there is an unhealthy version as well. The laissez-faire mindset can tend toward neglect and financial laziness. We are all called to be wise stewards of whatever resources God puts in our hands. It is one thing to work with a financially wise spouse or financial adviser, but it is another simply to waste what God gives you. Others can live with a defeatist mindset, self-sabotaging or never working toward financial goals because progress seems impossible.

If any of these unhealthy attitudes have become common, it is time to return to the Lord, surrender your finances to God, and ask God what he wants for your finances. If God is the owner and we are the money managers, we should try to honor God with our finances, even if that means starting today with whatever debt and bad decisions may have happened in the past.

Characteristics of a healthy laissez-faire mindset:

- Financially content and not driven by greed or materialism to accumulate more
- Deep trust in God in the area of finances
- Holding finances and materials with open hands for God to use

Characteristics of an unhealthy laissez-faire mindset:

- Paying no attention to finances to the point of neglect
- Giving up because any financial progress seems hopeless

Reflection Questions

On a scale of 1 to 10 (10 being the highest) how much do you think a laissez-faire mindset describes you? Which of these characteristics do you notice in your own life?

How have you been impacted by others with a laissez-faire mindset (family, friends, work colleagues, etc.)?

....

Lord, all I have is yours. Help me to trust you more and learn the secret of contentment. Show me when to work and when to rest, when to save and when to spend. Help me to pay off any debt and give generously to your Kingdom. Amen.

There are two ways of being rich—have a lot, or want very little. The latter way is the easier for most.
—Billy Graham

Pause and Reflect

As you look back at the past six days, what are you noticing?

Anything you want to confess or surrender to the Lord?

As you move forward on the journey, what is your hope or prayer?

Week 2

Childhood Money Memories

Day 7: Early Money Memories

Scripture: Proverbs 22:6

Start children off on the way they should go, and even
when they are old they will not turn from it.

Whenever Roz does premarital counseling for couples
about to embark on the adventure of marriage, he
covers various topics, such as communication, personality profile, family history, expectations, and finances. Financial
problems are one of the leading causes of divorce that put an added
strain on a marriage, and as the old saying goes, "opposites attract."
Often, one is a spender, and the other is a saver. However, one's view
of money is highly influenced by what he or she saw modeled growing up in his or her family of origin.

For example, Roz's parents immigrated from Sicily to America in
the late 1970s. For many reasons, Sicily relies on agriculture and has
remained underdeveloped compared to its counterpart in mainland
Italy. Roz's parents barely had elementary school educations before
they started working full-time. When they immigrated to America,
they had little money and did not speak the language. They worked
in factory jobs with subpar conditions, hoping to eventually buy
a home and a car and provide for their family. They succeeded in
their goals. However, it was a struggle, and unfortunately, Roz has
many memories of his father getting upset over the cost of items,
household spending, and constant worries about the future. He was
a saver. If he found a coin on the ground, he would stop and put it
in his pocket. Roz's dad would spend when he needed to, but it was
always something he did begrudgingly. Roz would have considered
his family below middle class, not exactly poor, though in some
sense others may have viewed them as such. His father had the best

intentions. He wanted to be responsible and upright, but in the process, a scarcity mentality prevailed. It drove a wedge between Roz's dad and the rest of the family.

Callie comes from a family of finance professionals, and even those who weren't finance experts by profession took an active interest. She was very much shaped by her parents but also by her grandparents. Callie's grandfather, whom she called "Honey," lived about an hour away, and he loved golf. He would take Callie and her brother hunting for golf balls in the woods and creek along the golf course. It was like an Easter Egg hunt year-round. If they found a golf ball, he'd give them a nickel, dime, or quarter for each one depending on the quality and condition of the golf ball. Callie loved having a way to earn some money as a kid. Soon, she and her brother started having lemonade stands and an allowance for doing chores around the house. Callie enjoyed "working" and earning money, even from a young age. As an adult, she still enjoys working (most days), being productive, and being compensated for what she accomplishes.

Reflection Questions

Reflect on your own childhood. What are some of your earliest financial memories?

How have the financial habits and attitudes of your parents or guardians influenced your current perspective on money and spending?

Roz and Callie come from two different backgrounds and now manage household finances together. How might you approach discussions about money with your spouse, significant other, or family, given the financial backgrounds and experiences each person brings?

....

Lord, you are the God of yesterday, today, and tomorrow. You know my past and how it shaped me, but you also hold my future. Please mold me into your image. Take what is good about what I learned as a child and grow it. Take what is unhealthy and heal it. In Jesus' name, amen.

Tell me and I forget, teach me and I may remember,
involve me and I learn.
—Benjamin Franklin

Day 8: Inherited Habits

Scripture: Romans 12:1-2

Therefore, I urge you, brothers and sisters, in view of God's mercy, to offer your bodies as a living sacrifice, holy and pleasing to God—this is your true and proper worship. Do not conform to the pattern of this world, but be transformed by the renewing of your mind. Then you will be able to test and approve what God's will is—his good, pleasing and perfect will.

What patterns or habits did you learn growing up from those who raised you? Those patterns are ones we often replicate unless we consciously make a change. Consider some of these habits that often get passed down:

- The guardian who would shop as a way of escaping from stress
- The parent who would buy an apology gift to make up for bad behavior
- The guardian who consistently checked their finances, balanced their checkbook, or reviewed credit card statements
- The adult in your life who always made the minimum payment and nothing more on debt
- The grandparent who always paid cash for everything they bought and refused to use any debt at all
- The parent who always leased their car
- The adult who always had the newest gadget
- The parent who threw big birthdays and always spoiled their kids

- The family who always went out to eat
- The family who always cooked their meals and only went out to eat on special occasions

The list could go on and on. Romans 12:1-2 reminds us that we are not our own. As Christians we are to offer all that we are and all that we have to God, refusing to conform to the patterns of this world. We are to be transformed by the renewing of our minds. When we are aware of the patterns we learned growing up and the patterns we see in God's Word, we can consciously choose which ones we want and which ones we need to change. We aren't doomed to repeat the past. We can experience the power of God's transforming work in our lives.

Reflection Questions

What patterns listed above and what other patterns did you observe growing up? Have you adopted any of these subconsciously? Are there any you have deliberately changed? Why or why not?

Make a list of the patterns you want to have that align with God's Word and a list of the patterns you want to stop that align with the patterns of the world.

What steps can you take to intentionally develop the godly habits on your list, and how can you seek accountability and support in breaking away from patterns that conform to the world?

....

God, forgive me for the areas I have conformed to the patterns of this world. I offer my whole self, including my finances, to you, as a living sacrifice. Transform me by the renewing of my mind, and align my life with your will. Amen.

Children have never been very good at listening to their elders, but they have never failed to imitate them.
—James Baldwin

Day 9: Between Cliché and Conviction

Scripture: 1 Corinthians 6:12

"I have the right to do anything," you say—but not every-thing is beneficial. "I have the right to do anything"—but I will not be mastered by anything.

The church in Corinth had some common sayings that they used to justify their actions. One was "I have the right to do anything." The apostle Paul wrote to them in 1 Corinthians 6, showing them the problem with the cliché they had internalized. He pointed out that not everything is beneficial, and that if you live by that mantra, you will be mastered by the sin you condone.

What financial mantras were common in your home growing up? Your environment can have a significant impact on your worldview and what you perceive as truth with those basic beliefs. Along the way, these beliefs and truths have been ingrained in us. These mantras and clichés are sayings we possibly now repeat to ourselves, our spouses and significant others, and/or our own children. Can you identify with any of these mantras and clichés:

- Money doesn't grow on trees.
- You can't take it with you when you go.
- Save for a rainy day.
- Money makes the world go round.
- Every penny counts.
- A penny saved is a penny earned.
- Live within your means.

- Cash is king.
- You've got to spend money to make money.

These all have elements of truth, but not all of them come from Scripture. Roz had bought into some of these clichés even though he was a Jesus follower. It was not until he took a biblically based financial course when he was engaged to Callie (it was a prerequisite to marrying her) that he learned valuable lessons. His new mantras about money started coming from the scriptures. Roz and Callie started memorizing verses such as Proverbs 22:7, "The borrower is slave to the lender." All of a sudden, something within Roz started to click. He did not have to give in to the worldly pressures of how to manage money. He learned money is not everything but simply a tool to be used in our society. Since going through the study and learning more about God's way of managing finances, he found himself quoting scriptures to friends and parishioners when the topic of money came up, not to beat them over the head, but to share what God has to say about something on which everyone has an opinion.

Reflection Questions

What are some of the clichés and mantras you have repeated to yourself and others?

How has scripture and the teachings of Jesus made any impact on your life when you think about finances?

....

God, please teach me your truth about finances. Where I have internalized worldly clichés, replace them with convictions based on your Word. Amen.

As we think, we change the physical nature of our brain. As we consciously direct our thinking, we can wire out toxic patterns of thinking and replace them with healthy thoughts.
—Dr. Caroline Leaf

Day 10: Godly Money Talks

Scripture: Colossians 4:6

> Let your conversation be always full of grace, seasoned with salt, so that you may know how to answer everyone.

How was money discussed in your home growing up? Were the conversations stressful? Peaceful? Nonexistent?

When we went through premarital counseling, the pastor told us the two things that were the best predictors of a long-lasting, healthy marriage were to have common beliefs/values and strong communication. Both affect how families and couples communicate around finances. Many families have an added layer of divorced parents or parents who were never married and now are separately working through the finances of caring for shared children.

Because of the importance of finances in paying for life, conversations around money can become heated. In some families, there can be a lot of secrets around money—separate bank accounts, hidden spending, or stashes of cash that the other spouse doesn't know about. Sometimes the main breadwinner makes most of the financial decisions in the family because of his or her income. This can generate mistrust. It can also be an area in which one spouse tries to control the other.

How your family communicated (or didn't communicate) around money can set a pattern that the next generation follows because that's what they have seen modeled or rejects because that's never how they want to act.

Reflection Questions

How was money discussed growing up in your home? Are these communication patterns you've continued or intentionally changed?

What type of conversations about money would you like to model for those around you? How do you think Jesus would handle money conversations?

....

God, please help my speech to always be gracious, seasoned with salt. Help me to communicate with others about finances in a way that is loving. Let my words reflect my love for you. Help me to model healthy financial conversations for others who see me. In Jesus' name, amen.

Handling money God's way is a lifelong process, not a one-time event.
—Howard Dayton

Day 11: Feelings about Finances

Scripture: Philippians 4:6-7

> Do not be anxious about anything, but in every situation,
> by prayer and petition, with thanksgiving, present your
> requests to God. And the peace of God, which transcends
> all understanding, will guard your hearts and your minds
> in Christ Jesus.

F eelings can often overwhelm facts. Memories with strong
feelings can stick with us more strongly. When those
memories come to mind, we often experience those emotions all over again.

When you think of money and your finances, what feelings
emerge? Was there anxiety around money growing up? Was there
satisfaction either with saving or spending? Was there fear of not
having enough? Disgust either with the lifestyle of the wealth or
the poor? Grief that leads to overspending? Perhaps even anger if
you or your family were wronged financially? What about peace?

Peace may be the last emotion most of us experience with finances because we have an advertising industry designed to make
us feel discontent. Those with a healthy laissez-faire mindset might
come closest to this peace and contentment. It requires a deep,
deep trust in God over money. It requires a focus on God that
washes away emotions of financial worry, anger, or fear, but also a
focus on God that washes away the strong sense of pride and satisfaction that can be found in money and possessions.

God wants us to find our worth in him alone, and God is constant in his love for us as his children. Our emotions may fluctuate when we focus on our finances, but when we focus on God, the Lord wants to overwhelm those emotions with his love for us.

Philippians 4:6-7 invites us to let go of anxiety (and you could insert any of those emotions here) and lift everything to God in prayer with thanksgiving. In the place of that anxiety, God promises his peace that surpasses all understanding, a peace that has the power to guard our hearts and minds in Christ Jesus. What situations do you need to lift up to God in prayer with thanksgiving today? Keep offering them to the Lord. Don't take them back.

Reflection Questions

What emotions do you experience as you think about your finances and possessions? Can you name some of those?

Growing up, what emotions were common in your household in general? What emotions were common around the topic of finances growing up?

....

God, if I'm honest, when financial topics come up, I feel
_____. I surrender these
emotions to you. Thank you for all of the resources I do have.
Thank you for the ways you've blessed me and provided
financially. Please continue providing, and guide me as I
steward these resources. I receive your peace that surpasses all
understanding. In Jesus' name, amen.

God is not against His people prospering, but
He is against their focusing on it.
—Larry Burkett

Day 12: Past Patterns, Present Choices

Scripture: 2 Corinthians 5:17

> Therefore, if anyone is in Christ, the new creation has come: The old has gone, the new is here!

We cannot control the past or what others have done to us, but our response can help shape the outcome of any situation. It can be hard to look at the past, and honestly, some of the memories can trigger the need to see a mental health specialist.

Here is the good news. While our past experiences shape us, they do not define us. The apostle Paul reminds us in 2 Corinthians 5:17 that "if anyone is in Christ, the new creation has come: The old has gone, the new is here!" In God's hands, our past becomes part of our testimony. There is power in knowing and naming our past because it helps us consciously choose what we want to continue from our past and what we want to change with God's help. Our response is an awakening by looking into the mirror and confronting the truth. The truth about ourselves stares us in the face, but very few are willing to respond with any significant change.

If you are feeling bad about your financial past, you are not alone. Finances are shaky for many of us, especially given the consumer debt load in the United States alone. Your past doesn't have to define your future. You cannot go back in time, but you can walk into the future with Jesus Christ as a new creation making positive changes.

Looking back at your past can help shape your present and future. Perhaps you had positive experiences in your past that have shaped you for the better, and because of that you steward resources well. The question then becomes, How can you walk alongside others who need help? Remember, we put our own oxygen mask on first before we can help others.

Reflection Questions

As you look back on your upbringing and past experiences with finances, what from these patterns, memories, beliefs, conversations, and feelings have you learned (either from positive experiences that you want to continue or negative that you want to avoid)? How do they impact the way you handle money today?

....

God, thank you for making me a new creation through Jesus Christ. Please breathe new life into my finances as well. Show me what in my past is positive that I should continue and what you would have me change to better reflect your Word and your will for my life. I surrender it all into your loving hands. In Jesus' name, amen.

Life is 10 percent what happens to us and 90 percent how we react to it.
–Charles R. Swindoll

Pause and Reflect

As you look back at the past six days, what are you noticing?

Anything you want to confess or surrender to the Lord?

As you move forward on the journey, what is your hope or prayer?

Learning from Experience

Day 13: Facing Financial Challenges

Scripture: Isaiah 41:10

So do not fear, for I am with you; do not be dismayed, for I am your God. I will strengthen you and help you; I will uphold you with my righteous right hand.

Roz was not much of a student growing up. He was the kid who got in trouble for wasting time, pulling pranks, or talking too much without permission. When all of his classmates and friends began talking about going to college, Roz ruled it out. It was not a dream he saw in his immediate context. Roz was encouraged by others to either work a factory job or enlist in the military, which seemed to be the only options for those in his hometown who were not going away to school. But through a lot of encouragement from a few people who took an interest in his future, he applied to only one school and got in. It was life-changing and transformative for Roz. It was exactly what he needed, but it was a private Christian college he could not afford. So, Roz took out loans and enlisted in the Marine Corps Reserves to receive the Montgomery GI Bill. However, he was left with over $50,000 in debt after college and graduate school. As soon as his six-month grace period was over, he began to pay off his loans. As a pastor, Roz did not have a high-paying job or any tangible assets. He was left with a feeling of hopelessness. He didn't want to save or plan because he thought, *What's the point? I am never going to be debt-free.*

Have you ever gone through a challenging financial situation? Perhaps you are in one right now. We talked about childhood experiences last week, but this week we are looking at some of our own experiences as we started making our own financial decisions. Often, they are connected. Either way, our own experiences with money as we journey into and through adulthood shape us. Overcoming challenges can bring us a sense of joy and accomplishment, but the repercussions of those situations can also burden us with shame, debt, poor credit, and hopelessness that impact our ability to move forward successfully.

In Isaiah 41:10, God promises, "So do not fear, for I am with you; do not be dismayed, for I am your God. I will strengthen you and help you; I will uphold you with my righteous right hand." Where do you need God's presence with you, God's strength and help, for God to uphold you with his righteous right hand? Many of these experiences aren't things we simply "get over" on our own. Ask God for help, and ask God if there are others you should approach for help as well.

Reflection Questions

Reflect on moments in your life when you've faced significant financial challenges. How did you navigate those situations?

How have these moments, even if they led to challenges like debt, shaped your character, faith, and relationship with God?

Isaiah 41:10 invites us to lean into God's presence, strength, and help. How can you do that during financial challenges? Are there specific areas in your financial journey today where you need to look to God for help?

....

God, it is hard not to be afraid and overwhelmed. Thank you for your promise to be with me, that I am never alone. Please strengthen and help me and uphold me with your righteous right hand. Amen.

God never uses anyone greatly until He tests them deeply.
—A. W. Tozer

Day 14: Growing through the Good

Scripture: 2 Corinthians 8:1-5

And now, brothers and sisters, we want you to know about the grace that God has given the Macedonian churches. In the midst of a very severe trial, their overflowing joy and their extreme poverty welled up in rich generosity. For I testify that they gave as much as they were able, and even beyond their ability. Entirely on their own, they urgently pleaded with us for the privilege of sharing in this service to the Lord's people. And they exceeded our expectations: They gave themselves first of all to the Lord, and then by the will of God also to us.

Serving in ministry, we have always wanted to live in the same neighborhood where our church was located. This can be financially stretching, because every move costs money. There is a cost to buy and sell houses. When we first got married, Callie owned a beautiful home in Lexington, Kentucky, but it wasn't in the same neighborhood as our downtown church locations. A house came on the market that was right between our two downtown church sites, so we looked at it. Built in 1892, it needed many updates and it reeked of cat pee when you entered the front door. Still, we felt called to move there.

We listed our house for sale, but it wasn't selling. We went ahead and bought the new house, taking on a second mortgage, and started fixing up the new house. It turned out pouring a gallon of vinegar between the floorboards took care of the cat pee smell! At the same time, we felt called to increase our giving to church beyond what financially made sense. Still, our old house wasn't selling.

The new house repairs were complete, and as we were preparing to move and praying for options, a buyer approached us just as the listing was about to expire. We were able to stay in our old house during the renovation of our new house, and the old house sold just when we no longer needed it.

Less than a year later, God called us to Dayton, Ohio. Another move! Why would God have us move when we had just felt led to move less than a year before? But then we realized we could rent out our downtown home and easily cover our costs in a way we could not have with our nice house in the suburbs. The move we had made a year earlier prepared us financially to be able to move to Dayton. Then after going to Ohio, a buyer approached us to buy our Lexington house without us even having to list it! We saw God provide financially in ways we could never have imagined or planned.

Just as negative money experiences can shape us, so can positive money experiences. Have you ever seen God provide in a miraculous way? The Macedonian churches sure did. As Paul describes them in 2 Corinthians 8:1-5, he notes their incredible generosity and joy, even giving in the midst of affliction and poverty. He says, "They gave as much as they were able, and even beyond their ability" (verse 3). God allowed them to give beyond their ability.

These positive financial experiences can grow our faith. Sometimes it's in the generosity of a stranger who blesses us. Sometimes it is in the earning of a first paycheck. Some businesses frame the first dollar they earn because it marks the start of a financial venture. Others remember opening their first savings account. God can do financial miracles that have a profound impact on our life and faith.

Reflection Questions

Whether they feel ordinary or miraculous, what positive money experiences have impacted you?

How have you seen God provide financially in your life? As you reflect on those experiences, how do they impact your approach or feelings toward your financial situation today?

....

God, thank you for all the ways you have provided in my life. Thank you for the miracles and the signs of everyday faithfulness. Help me to stay in that posture of gratitude as I lift up my current financial position to you. Thank you for your continued provision and guidance. As you bless me, help me to be a blessing to others as well. Amen.

What you do with your resources in this life i
s your autobiography of what you believe about God.
—Randy Alcorn

Day 15: Godly Victory

Scripture: Philippians 3:14

> I press on toward the goal to win the prize for which God has called me heavenward in Christ Jesus.

Dave Ramsey has come up with a fun way to celebrate the financial victory of becoming debt-free. He invites those who have become debt-free in the past six months to come on *The Dave Ramsey Show* and give a "debt-free scream." It's a way of celebrating the moment that individuals and families are no longer enslaved by debt to their lender. They are free!

Those financial victories can shape us. They can motivate us on the journey. They can also become a stumbling block if we become overly focused on the numbers. The key difference is, who or what is leading your financial journey?

When we lean into God for strength, wisdom, and provision, those victories can grow our faith. When we lean into our own independence and hard work, the temptation can be to think we don't need God. An eternal relationship with God through Christ Jesus is the goal. Finances are a tool on the journey.

Consider the following financial victories. Have you experienced any of these? What other ones have you had in your life? Where was God in those?

- a big gift, inheritance, or bonus
- getting a promotion
- paying off a debt
- reaching a savings goal, such as a down payment for a home or an apartment, paying for a car or computer, building an emergency fund, saving for retirement, helping a child afford college

- beginning to tithe 10 percent of what you earn to invest in God's Kingdom or making a generous gift that stretched you and brought you joy

As you think about the financial victories you've had, is there one you are working toward right now? Write it down and give it to God. Invite God into the process.

Reflection Questions

What are some of the financial victories you've celebrated? Where was God in the process? Were you leaning on God or your own willpower?

As you work toward your current financial goals, how can you ensure that God remains at the center of the process, guiding your decisions and actions?

....

God, you are the ultimate prize. I want my whole life to point toward you. Please lead me in my finances toward goals that you place on my heart, but help me to keep you always as my ultimate focus. In Jesus' name, amen.

Winning at money is 80 percent behavior and 20 percent head knowledge.
—Dave Ramsey

Day 16: Christ-Centered Money Makeover

Scripture: Isaiah 43:19

"See, I am doing a new thing! Now it springs up; do you not perceive it? I am making a way in the wilderness and streams in the wasteland."

Humans have long been fascinated by the metamorphosis of the butterfly. The caterpillar forms itself into a chrysalis, enclosing itself in a cocoon. When it emerges from the chrysalis, the caterpillar looks like a completely new creation. It is now a butterfly, with beautiful wings. This formerly landbound creature can now fly!

Have you experienced a similar transformation? When you look back, do you marvel at what God has done in your life? It's easy to become critical of where we are now and forget the transformations we've gone through. Or perhaps you are in the cocoon right now, working to break out, to spread your wings and fly.

As you look back, have you experienced a major change financially? Were you once the person who never budgeted and now you are spending intentionally, making progress toward financial goals? Were you once spending to keep up with those around you, and now you are walking in contentment, enjoying what you have? Are you in recovery from a spending addiction? Did you make the leap from rarely giving or "tipping God" to consistently giving a percentage of your income back to God? Have you moved from making minimum payments on credit cards to paying them off monthly?

Those money changes are part of our testimony. Second Corinthians 5:17 tells us, "Therefore, if anyone is in Christ, the new creation has come: The old has gone, the new is here!" And in Isaiah 43:19, God reminds us, "See, I am doing a new thing! Now it springs up; do you not perceive it? I am making a way in the wilderness and streams in the wasteland." Transformation is possible, and when we experience that freedom of being a new creation in Christ, the old version of ourselves has no hold over us. We may still be coming out of those past financial mistakes, but they no longer define who we are. Poverty is no longer our shame or our identity, because Jesus says, "Blessed are the poor in spirit, for theirs is the kingdom of heaven" (Matthew 5:3). We have an eternal inheritance. That means wealth no longer defines us.

As you walk in your identity as a new creation in Christ and the new thing God is doing, let the financial changes you want to make flow from that identity. Wealth is not the goal. Christ is. As we follow Christ and make Jesus the goal we pursue, our past financial mistakes lose their grip on us, and we learn to hold all things with an open hand, faithfully managing all that God has entrusted to us, but not letting any of it define us. We have a new identity in Christ.

Reflection Questions

Where have you experienced a metamorphosis in your faith and finances? Where do you see God starting to do something new, even if it's just a hint?

How does your new identity in Christ shape the way you want to handle your finances differently in the future? Is there a new thing God wants to do in your finances?

....

God, thank you for your transforming work in my life and the area of my finances. As I look at the changes I want to make, help me to remain grateful for the changes that have already come. I celebrate those with you. Thank you for the new things you are doing in my life, for making a way where there seems to be no way. In Jesus' name, amen.

Transformation is a process, and as life happens there are tons of ups and downs. It's a journey of discovery—there are moments on mountaintops and moments in deep valleys of despair.
—Rick Warren

Day 17: Attitude Indicator

Scripture: Matthew 6:24

"No one can serve two masters. Either you will hate the one and love the other, or you will be devoted to the one and despise the other. You cannot serve both God and money."

Have you checked your attitude lately toward money? Airplanes have what is called an attitude indicator. It lets the pilot know the plane's position relative to the earth's horizon. It tells the pilot whether the plane is climbing or descending, rolling to the left or to the right. Important all the time, this navigation instrument is especially essential when visibility is limited or nonexistent.

If your heart had an attitude indicator to let you know your position relative to money, what would it say?

The Holy Spirit and the Word of God function as our spiritual attitude indicators when it comes to wealth. Out of Jesus' thirty-nine parables, eleven are focused on the topic of money. Matthew 6:24 is an attitude check when it comes to the love of money. Money can easily become an idol, just as a plane without an attitude indicator can drift dangerously off course. If the position of money in our life becomes the number one priority in our heart, it begins to rival the attention we give to Jesus.

Many of us struggle with idolizing money. Idolatry can show up as greed or the constant chase and pursuit of money, but idolatry can also creep in with the constant worry and tension around how we use money. Money is simply a tool, and there is a need for it to be managed well, but there is a need for a healthy balance. Do we control our finances or does our need for money control us? If we let it, money can control our attitude, emotions, and how much attention we give it, whether it is too much importance or not enough. If you struggle, you are not alone. As one person said, after we come to Christ, the hardest conversion to follow is the checkbook conversion.

Reflection Questions

How would you describe your attitude and attention toward money today? Do you lean more toward worry or the pursuit of more money?

What helps keep your attitude in check? If it's scripture, is there a particular Bible verse that helps you?

....

God, please check my attitude toward money. Show me where I need an adjustment, and forgive me for where I have gotten off course. I surrender my finances and possessions to you once again. You alone are Lord, and I want to worship you alone. Amen.

Money often costs too much.
—Ralph Waldo Emerson

Day 18: God-Guided Goals

Scripture: Proverbs 16:3

> Commit to the LORD whatever you do, and he will establish your plans.

Scripture: Proverbs 16:9

> In their hearts humans plan their course, but the LORD establishes their steps.

When Callie meets with financial coaching clients, one of the early questions she asks is, "What are your short-term and long-term financial goals?" Goals give us direction. Without a goal, we tend to aimlessly work on a little something over here and a little something over there without working toward anything in particular.

Goal setting comes more naturally to some financial mindsets than others, and some mindsets greatly prioritize some goals over others. For example, someone with a security mindset will tend to set savings goals. Someone with a collector mindset will more likely work toward a purchase. The person with a benevolence mindset will work toward a goal of blessing others. The laissez-faire mindset makes goal setting hard. The person with a carpe diem mindset would most likely work toward a big trip or a bucket list experience.

The big thing with all of them is asking these more important questions:

- God, what do you want me to focus on?
- Lord, what financial goals would you have me set?

Proverbs 16:9 encourages, "In their hearts humans plan their course, but the LORD establishes their steps." We may come up with our own plans for execution, but if we follow Christ, it should be the Lord who directs our steps. What are those goals God has for you? Goals to become debt-free? Goals to increase your giving, support a missionary, work in ministry? Goals to build an emergency fund, save for a big purchase, for college, for retirement? Goals to live within a budget, start a business, fund a ministry?

Once we hear from the Lord, those plans should be given to the Lord in prayer. Proverbs 16:3 offers this wisdom: "Commit to the LORD whatever you do, and he will establish your plans." Keep committing those goals to God and working toward them with diligence. Setbacks happen, but goals keep us focused and moving in the right direction.

Reflection Questions

What are your current financial goals? How do they align with your personal mindset and priorities? Have you taken the time to discern if these goals align with God's purpose for your life?

Considering Proverbs 16:9, how can you ensure that while you make plans, you remain open to God's guidance and direction in your financial journey? Are there any specific areas where you feel the need for clearer direction from the Lord?

As you think about the five financial mindsets, which one resonates most with you? How can you leverage the strengths of that mindset while also seeking God's guidance to ensure your goals are in line with his will?

....

God, I commit these goals to you. Please direct my steps and guide me. If any of these goals need to change, please show me. I want you to lead me on the path you have for me. In Jesus' name, amen.

Align your financial goals with God's heart, and you'll find purpose in every dollar you steward.
—Rachel Cruze

Pause and Reflect

As you look back at the past six days, what are you noticing?

Anything you want to confess or surrender to the Lord?

As you move forward on the journey, what is your hope or prayer?

Financial Healing

Day 19: Breaking Financial Lies

Scripture: John 10:10

> "The thief comes only to steal and kill and destroy; I have come that they may have life and have it to the full."

C allie grew up wrestling with guilt for having nice things. She knew Matthew 19:24 said, "Again I tell you, it is easier for a camel to go through the eye of a needle than for someone who is rich to enter the kingdom of God." So, she rejected the lie that she needed to have nice things in order to have worth. However, Satan is tricky. He is called the deceiver, the father of lies, and in John 10:10 "the thief [who] comes only to steal and kill and destroy." Since the one lie of needing to have nice things didn't work, the lie that caught Callie was the lie that she *couldn't* enjoy nice things. Callie has some of the benevolence mindset that you may hear about here.

Depending on your money mindset, childhood money memories, and adult experiences, you may have different lies you've internalized. Don't be ashamed, but also don't let those linger.

While the devil tries to use those lies to steal, kill, and destroy, Jesus goes on to say, "I have come that they may have life, and have it to the full." Jesus came to set us free from those lies and from our sins so that we can have abundant life.

The first step is uncovering those lies. Ask God to bring those lies into the light of God's truth and grace. Take a look at some of the common financial lies listed below, but also consider others you've learned along the way:

- Contract theology/Prosperity Gospel: If I give to God monetarily, I am going to automatically get blessed with material possessions.

77

- I can't have or enjoy nice things.
- Faith in God will lead to financial gain. All you have to do is believe (but no action on your part is required).
- I have to prove my worth by what I earn and what I have.
- Wealth is a sign of God's favor, and poverty is a curse.
- No matter how hard I work I will never be debt-free or have financial security.
- I can't.
- I am not enough.
- I will never have enough.

Reflection Questions

What lies have you believed when it comes to finances?

How has your outlook changed as a result of placing faith in Christ?

....

God, please uncover the lies in my life. Bring each untruth into the light, so I can name those lies for what they are. I want your truth. Amen.

Renewing our minds with God's truth is the key to breaking free from financial myths. As we align our thinking with Christ's teachings, we can discern His will for our finances and experience true freedom.
—Ron Blue

Day 20: Planting Truths, Uprooting Lies

Scripture: John 8:31-32

> To the Jews who had believed him, Jesus said, "If you hold to my teaching, you are really my disciples. Then you will know the truth, and the truth will set you free.

Have you ever fought a losing battle with a garden full of weeds? You pulled weeds only to have them come back again and again, so the cycle repeats. One thing many gardeners have learned is to replace those weeds with something stronger. A thick and beautiful ground cover makes it hard for weeds to get through. Sure, one or two may appear, but not with the previous strength.

So it is with getting rid of lies in your life. As you name the lies, it is like pulling out the weeds. This is the first step. But they will come back if you don't replace them with something stronger. In John 8:31-32, Jesus offers us a truth that will make us free, and that truth comes from God's Word. What truths do you need to plant in your heart to replace those lies?

For example:

- Lie: "I am not enough."
- Truth: "My grace is sufficient for you, for my power is made perfect in weakness" (2 Corinthians 12:9).

- Lie: "I will never have enough."
- Truth: "I have learned to be content whatever the circumstances. I know what it is to be in need, and I know what it is to have plenty" (Philippians 4:11-12).

- Lie: "I can't."
- Truth: "I can do all this through him who gives me strength" (Philippians 4:13).

- Lie: "I need more wealth to find security."
- Truth: "I will say of the LORD, 'He is my refuge and my fortress, my God, in whom I trust'" (Psalm 91:2).

Pick a scripture that contains a truth to replace each lie that you have internalized. Place it somewhere you will see it regularly. Try to memorize it, so that anytime the lie comes up, the truth will be like that thick and beautiful ground cover that keeps the weeds out, and even if a few lies manage to get through, they can be easily removed.

Reflection Questions

As you look back at the lies you named yesterday, what truth from God do you need to internalize in place of that lie? Take a moment to look up scripture verses that contain those truths. Write them here and read through them a couple of times each.

There is power in praying scripture. Take your scripture verses and write them out as a prayer. (Example from Psalm 91:2: God, you are my refuge and my fortress; my God, in whom I trust. You are the source of my security.)

....

Pray the prayer you wrote today or pray this one if you are still searching for the truth to replace the lie you've uprooted:

God, I know you are the truth. Please speak to me through your Word that I may know the truth and be set free from the lies I have believed for far too long. I want to walk with you in freedom and truth.

In the garden of our minds, God's truth serves as the vibrant flowers that suffocate the weeds of deception and doubt.
—Ann Voskamp

Day 21: Liberation from Financial Chains

Scripture: 2 Corinthians 10:3-5

> For though we live in the world, we do not wage war as the world does. The weapons we fight with are not the weapons of the world. On the contrary, they have divine power to demolish strongholds. We demolish arguments and every pretension that sets itself up against the knowledge of God, and we take captive every thought to make it obedient to Christ.

Are there strongholds or addictions holding you back in your financial journey? We like to think that we are fully in control, but sometimes there are things spiritually and emotionally holding us back that can't be overcome by sheer willpower.

Callie struggles with perfectionism and people pleasing. In the area of finances, it made her afraid to take any financial risks or do anything that didn't line up with the world's ways of wise financial management. She's in active recovery from both, but that couldn't start until she named them and started bringing those to God. As God became bigger in her life, the strongholds of what others thought and doing things the "right" way began to lose their power.

The good news is this: "The weapons we fight with are not the weapons of the world. On the contrary, they have divine power to demolish strongholds" (2 Corinthians 10:4). We have something greater than our will. We have the Holy Spirit. Through prayer we can identify and pray down spiritual strongholds that have been holding us back for years. With the higher power of Jesus Christ, we can overcome addiction. Consider some of the following implications of strongholds:

- Shopping can become an addiction, especially with the ease of shopping online.

- Fear can hold us back.

- The need for the approval of parents, even if they were absent or if they are now dead, can continue to control our actions.

- Gambling addiction can keep us from moving forward financially.

- Drugs and alcohol can deplete all our savings and keep us from productive work.

- Negative, defeating words that we've let take root inside can cause us to give up before we ever get started.

- There is power in naming. In recovery, the fourth step is to "make a searching and fearless moral inventory."[1] With the boldness of the Holy Spirit, can you ask God to look with you to see what strongholds and addictions are holding you back? As you uncover each one, lift it to the Lord. Ask for forgiveness, freedom, and healing from the One who is more than able and loves you unconditionally.

---

1. American Addiction Centers Editorial Staff, "Alcoholics Anonymous Step 4: Make a Moral Inventory," Recovery.org, accessed February 6, 2024, https://recovery.org/alcoholics-anonymous/step-4/.

Reflection Questions

Reflect on your financial journey thus far. Are there specific strongholds or patterns of behavior that you recognize as obstacles to your financial well-being? How have these impacted your decisions and overall financial health?

Considering 2 Corinthians 10:4, how can you actively engage the divine power of the Holy Spirit to confront and overcome these financial strongholds? What specific steps can you take to invite God's intervention in these areas?

The act of naming and acknowledging our strongholds is a powerful step toward liberation. As you identify these strongholds, how can you create a consistent prayer strategy to seek God's forgiveness, freedom, and healing in each area?

....

*God, thank you that I don't have to face any of these
strongholds or addictions alone. You have the divine power to
demolish these strongholds. Tear them down in Jesus' name.
I want to be fully free to follow you in all areas of my life.
Amen.*

*The victorious Christian escapes from these strongholds by identifying
every false theory, every human philosophy and every prideful thought
that have controlled us and replaces it with Truth. Money will not
destroy a financial stronghold. Only by the power of God's Spirit
and Word can we escape these false philosophies
that hold us back from God's plan.*
—Chuck Bentley

Day 22: God's Financial Rest

Scripture: Matthew 11:28-30

"Come to me, all you who are weary and burdened, and I will give you rest. Take my yoke upon you and learn from me, for I am gentle and humble in heart, and you will find rest for your souls. For my yoke is easy and my burden is light."

Sometimes trying to take care of finances can feel like a heavy burden. Stuff keeps breaking, wearing out, and needing replacement. It can feel like an uphill battle to get finances in order.

In Matthew 11:28-30, Jesus offers the beautiful invitation, "Come to me, all you who are weary and burdened, and I will give you rest." Ah, rest. OK, Jesus, here are all my heavy burdens. However, He doesn't stop there. Jesus offers us his yoke, which is easy, and his burden, which is light. He invites us to learn from his way of doing things. There is still work to be done, but Jesus invites us to work a different way.

What is that different way to approach our finances? Just as each lie that was uncovered needed to be replaced with truth from the Word of God, the strongholds and addictive behaviors need to be replaced with healthy spiritual disciplines. The spiritual disciplines are things like prayer, silence, scripture reading, simplicity, worship, giving, journaling, giving thanks, confession, and service. Look at the strongholds and addictive behaviors you named. Can you identify a spiritual discipline to practice that will help with each one or with multiple?

For example:

- Shopping addiction: Start making a gratitude list of at least five things you are thankful for each day.

- Fear: Journal and pray, confessing to God your fear, and asking God for strength.

- Approval seeking: Read scriptures that remind you of God's love for you.

- Gambling, drugs, or alcohol addiction: Find a sponsor and join a recovery group that allows you to practice confession and find support from others on the journey with you.

- Negative/defeating words: Worship God and turn your attention from problems to the God who is greater than anything you face.

The disciplines are all designed to take the focus off of ourselves and turn our attention to loving God and loving others. They are all active work, but it is a yoke that is easy and a burden that is light. How is God inviting you to experience rest and a gentler way of working?

Reflection Questions

Reflect on the financial burdens you currently carry. How do they impact your daily life and your relationship with God? How can you actively lay these burdens at Jesus' feet and seek his guidance in navigating them?

As you look at the strongholds and addictive behaviors you named on Day 21, list at least one spiritual discipline for each. It might be one of the disciplines listed above or another practice that helps you love God and others and lessens the power of the stronghold in your life.

....

God, I am worn out. I can't do this on my own. Help me to work with you instead of carrying this all on my own. Show me the spiritual disciplines that will teach me a new way of working on my finances. I want your yoke that is easy and your burden that is light. Amen.

Disciplines are not the answer; they only lead us to the Answer.
—Richard Foster

Day 23: Beyond Symptoms

Scripture: Psalm 139:23-24 (NRSV)

Search me, O God, and know my heart; test me and know my thoughts. See if there is any wicked way in me, and lead me in the way everlasting.

When Callie was in her midtwenties, she began to get headaches. She would ignore them, try ibuprofen, or drink some caffeine. That worked at times, but then she started noticing the patterns. They occurred when she had been driving for a while; when she was in church, trying to pay attention to the preacher preaching (her handsome husband, Rosario); and when she was sitting across a table, trying to make eye contact during a conversation. Could it be that the headaches were related to her eyes? Callie went to the eye doctor, and sure enough, she needed glasses.

How often do we try to treat symptoms without stopping to notice the underlying problem? This does not pertain only to our physical health. We could ask the same question about our financial and spiritual health.

Consider the couple who tries to hide their spending from each other or spends money to get even when they are mad at one another. There is an underlying need for forgiveness and reconciliation that goes deeper than the spending.

What about the adult who struggles with giving and trusting a church or nonprofit because he or she has been betrayed by someone who wounded him or her deeply, which has led to challenges trusting God and others?

Think about the person who was told he or she was worthless and is now trying to prove his or her worth through a job title, wealth, or possessions.

Healing can take time, but the first step is naming what needs to be healed or forgiven. Who or what hurt you? Depending on the level of hurt, it may be extremely wise to engage a mental health professional, therapist, spiritual director, or mentor.

In Psalm 139:23-24, we find a powerful prayer inviting the Holy Spirit to guide us, to reveal the truth, and to heal us. Will you stop and slowly pray this prayer now one line at a time, adding your own words with each line?

> "Search me, O God"
> "and know my heart"
> "test me and know my thoughts"
> "See if there is any wicked way in me"
> "and lead me in the way everlasting."

Reflection Questions

Reflect on a time when you addressed a symptom in your life without delving deeper into the root cause. How did this approach impact your overall well-being, and what did you learn from the experience?

Consider your financial and spiritual habits. Are there any patterns or behaviors that might be indicative of deeper, unresolved issues or wounds? How can you take steps to address and heal these underlying concerns?

As you ponder Psalm 139:23-24, what areas of your life need deeper healing? How can you invite God as the Great Physician into these areas?

....

God, help me uncover what lies underneath the symptoms and help me bring it to you. I want your real healing for the underlying causes. Please breathe new life in me and lead me in the way everlasting. Amen.

To experience true transformation, we must have the courage to con-front the underlying issues beneath the surface symptoms.
—Brené Brown

.

Day 24: Abundant Healing Steps

Scripture: Luke 6:37-38 (NRSV)

"Do not judge, and you will not be judged; do not condemn, and you will not be condemned. Forgive, and you
will be forgiven; give, and it will be given to you. A good
measure, pressed down, shaken together, running over, will
be put into your lap, for the measure you give will be the
measure you get back."

We have small kids, and periodically we will try to go
for a walk or bike ride. When the kids have energy
and are motivated to reach the destination, we move
forward quickly. Other times, they are tired, and we spend most
of our time encouraging them and helping them move forward. "I
know you are tired, but once we get to the house, you can relax and
have a snack." "Do you want to race?" We try just about anything.

Worst of all though is when they have a meltdown, kicking and
screaming, refusing to move forward, and trying to go backward. If
we really have to get home quickly, we can end up dragging a bike
and pulling a kid in full-on tantrum mode who is trying to run in
the opposite direction. "Why did we go on this walk again?"

Healing is a journey. Sometimes it moves quickly. Other times
it seems to move slowly. The biggest factor is whether we are working with our heavenly Father or fighting against him. God knows
how to lovingly work with us when we are ready, but when we fight
it, we stay stuck in our unhealth. How do we fight it?

- Unforgiveness.
- Refusing to ask for help (from God and others).

- Continuing to blame others for all our problems rather than examining our own hearts.

- Avoiding counseling, when mental health healing is needed.

- Self-medicating.

- Pretending everything is fine when we know it's not.

In Luke 6:37-38, Jesus shows what happens when we work with God in the healing journey, moving in the same direction instead of fighting it: "Do not judge, and you will not be judged; do not condemn, and you will not be condemned. Forgive, and you will be forgiven; give, and it will be given to you. A good measure, pressed down, shaken together, running over, will be put into your lap, for the measure you give will be the measure you get back"(NRSV).

When we take a step toward healing with God, whether that's choosing not to judge, not to condemn, to forgive, to give, to seek help, to be real, God meets us there. It doesn't mean the journey will be free from pain, but we are walking with our heavenly Father, who loves us and is our ever-present help in time of need.

Reflection Questions

As you think about the areas that need continued healing, what actions are you taking that work with God in the process?

If you are really honest, what is hardest to let go of? Are there areas where forgiveness, asking for help, or being vulnerable about mistakes is hard? What one step can you take to release those to God?

....

God, this is really hard. I want healing, but it's painful at times. You know what I can handle and when. Please lead me and keep encouraging me when I want to quit. I need you. In Jesus' name, please heal me physically, mentally, spiritually, financially, and relationally. Amen.

The first step towards getting somewhere
is to decide you're not going to stay where you are.
—J. P. Morgan

Pause and Reflect

As you look back at the past six days, what are you noticing?

Anything you want to confess or surrender to the Lord?

As you move forward on the journey, what is your hope or prayer?

Moving Forward Financially

Day 25: Purposeful Priorities

Scripture: Joshua 24:15

"But if serving the LORD seems undesirable to you, then choose for yourselves this day whom you will serve, whether the gods your ancestors served beyond the Euphrates, or the gods of the Amorites, in whose land you are living. But as for me and my household, we will serve the LORD."

What do you value most in life? Many will list their faith and family at the top of the list. The challenge is our spending of time and money do not always reflect that. Over time things can shift.

In Joshua 24, the Israelites are renewing their covenant before the Lord. Joshua led the people into the promised land, but now they are entering a time of peace, and Joshua knows that it is easy for focus to drift. Joshua is now older and nearing the end of his life, so he draws all the Israelite leaders together, reminds them of all the Lord has done for them, and then challenges them to "choose . . . this day whom you will serve." It is time for them to choose how they will align their life. Will their life worship the Lord or the gods of those around them? For Joshua, the decision is clear, "As for me and my household, we will serve the Lord."

As you align your finances, it is important to determine what you value most. If serving God, taking care of your family, caring for the poor, investing in future leaders, being a light in your workplace or community, and stewarding God's creation, for example, are important for you, does your budget reflect that? Hopefully, God is at the top of your list, but as you work your way down to some of the specifics of God's calling on your life, what is a priority for you? What are your life goals as you live out your faith on this earth?

Reflection Questions

Take a moment to prayerfully list some of those values and goals below:

Consider Joshua's challenge to the Israelites. Where do you need to reevaluate any of those values and "choose . . . this day whom you will serve"?

....

God, not my will, but yours be done. I lift all these things to you. Above all else, I want to serve and honor you. Amen.

The principle of 'first things first' applies to our finances as well. When we prioritize our spending according to our values, we position ourselves to live a life of purpose and impact.
—Andy Stanley

Day 26: Financial Alignment

Scripture: Proverbs 3:5-6

> Trust in the Lord with all your heart
> and lean not on your own understanding;
> in all your ways submit to him,
> and he will make your paths straight.

We try to take care of our cars, but sometimes it seems as if car maintenance can become ridiculously expensive. Are some of those maintenance items *really* necessary? One of those regular items that can be tempting to skip is checking and adjusting wheel alignment. In the short term, it may not make a big difference, but over the long term, it can cause tires, steering, and suspension to wear out faster, causing even bigger expenses. If wheels are out of alignment, the tire won't touch the road fully and at the correct angle, which can impact steering and how your car drives. Have you ever been driving straight and felt your car trying to drift to one side or the other?

Even more important than wheel alignment is the alignment of our life and finances with God's Word. Being out of alignment a little bit might not seem like a big deal in the short term, but over the long term, it can lead to prioritizing the wrong things, neglecting what is most important, and wear you out spiritually and financially. All of this can have major financial and life consequences.

Proverbs 3:5-6 shows us how to get back into alignment when something is off that is making us drift to one side or the other. "Trust in the Lord with all your heart and lean not on your own understanding; in all your ways submit to him, and he will make your paths straight."

Reflection Questions

Last time, you listed your values, life goals, and God's calling on your life in specific ways. Today, it's time for an alignment check. Take a look at the way you spend your time, finances, and energy. Go through your credit card and/or bank statement. What does your spending say you value? Look at your calendar. What does your time say you value? Consider where your thoughts have been lately. What is consuming your mental or physical energy? How does your list compare to yesterday's list?

Now, invite God to bring your life back in alignment with God's plan for you. Take a moment to pray Proverbs 3:5-6:

"Lord, help me to trust you with all of my heart and not lean on my own understanding."

Take a moment to confess some of the areas in which you have not trusted God with your whole heart and/or where you have depended on your own understanding instead.

"God, I submit my time, my finances, my energy, everything to You. Not my will, but yours be done. Please realign my life and make my path straight."

What one or two changes is God leading you to make to bring your life back in alignment with God's Word, the values and goals God has given you, the calling God has on your life?

....

God, please align my finances and all areas of my life with you. I want my spending, giving, and saving to reflect your love and Kingdom priorities to the world around me. Please realign my life with your will and your Word. In Jesus' name, amen.

When you align yourself with God's purpose as described in the Scriptures, something special happens to your life.
—Bono

Day 27: As Iron Sharpens Iron

Scripture: Proverbs 27:17

As iron sharpens iron, so one person sharpens another.

W e live in an individualistic culture. It is hard to form meaningful relationships where we can be transparent and authentic with one another. Even among Jesus' followers, it is hard to admit weakness and even ask for help. However, we cannot live this life in isolation or alone. If we are having any struggle, especially falling short in the area of finances, are we keeping this to ourselves or are we talking to someone about it? The old saying remains true, "We are only as sick as our secrets." In the walls of Alcoholics Anonymous, those seeking recovery are charged with finding a sponsor and checking in regularly with that sponsor to share struggles and victories and to work the 12 steps. It is no coincidence that AA and other recovery communities make better disciples than most churches, because we have failed to form relationships and seek mentors.

In the area of finances, your "sponsor" could be your spouse if you are married, a trusted friend, or a financial adviser. It is important to find a person who is safe, who won't use what you share against you in any way. It should be someone trustworthy who wants you to succeed.

Another way to look at support is in the form of accountability. One option is to use technology to track your spending. You can do so with hundreds of mobile apps at your disposal. This often makes accountability with another human easier when spending is visible. When Roz does premarital counseling or even one-on-one discipleship, he always asks individuals how they are doing in managing the resources that God has blessed them with. Discipleship involves all areas of one's life.

Reflection Questions

Who can you be real and transparent with in your struggles and victories regarding any issue, especially in finances?

If you have not formed those types of relationships, can you identify the barriers that have stopped you in the past?

What is one step you can take today in being open with another person?

....

Almighty God, help me to be open and transparent with the people you have placed in my life. I know that I cannot live this life alone. As you sharpen me, help me to look more like Jesus today than I did yesterday. I want to allow others to help me in the areas of my life where I am weak. Please help me to find those people. In Jesus' name, amen.

Vulnerability is not winning or losing; it's having the courage to show up and be seen when we have no control over the outcome.
—Brené Brown

Day 28: Rejoice in Every Victory

Scripture: Philippians 4:4

Rejoice in the Lord always. I will say it again: Rejoice!

The apostle Paul's words to the Philippians about rejoicing and celebrating in the Lord are written from his prison cell on death row in Rome. A few verses later, he shares how he has learned the secret of contentment whether in plenty or in want; and because of that, Paul knows he can do all things through Christ who gives him strength (Philippians 4:11-13).

Paul teaches us to celebrate in the Lord no matter what we face. We are instructed to rejoice no matter the circumstance. However, in the rat race we call life, we can get so stuck on accomplishing a goal that we don't take time to celebrate the smallest of milestones. Instead, we just move on to the next thing we must do. If you are trying to lose weight, rejoice over every pound lost and celebrate it (probably not with an ice cream sundae). If you have paid off one debt, take the time to celebrate instead of worrying about the rest you need to pay off.

When Roz graduated from seminary, he was left with $50,000 worth of debt. He did the steady plodding of paying off one small loan after another, paying extra each month, until the day he was able to be completely free from student loans. It was a huge accomplishment. Of course, he kept thinking about the other things he had to work for, such as saving, retirement, and future purchases. This is where the support comes in, because Callie reminded Roz to stop and celebrate how God was faithful and blessed the work that went into paying off the debt. We celebrated together along the way, giving thanks to God. Don't forget to rejoice!

Reflection Questions

How easy or hard is it for you to celebrate when you have made major progress on a goal or even accomplished it? What makes it challenging at times?

Is there anything that you have accomplished that you can celebrate right now with a friend, a family member, or your spouse? What is a reasonable way that you would enjoy celebrating progress or an accomplishment?

....

Dear Jesus, thank you for enabling me with your power to do the work you have called me to in this season. Help me not to be so goal and results driven that I forget to celebrate all that you have done in me and through me. I want to honor you with my struggles and even when I experience victory. I want to rejoice in you! In Jesus' name, amen.

We may encounter many defeats, but we must not be defeated. It may even be necessary to encounter the defeat, so that we can know who we are. So that we can see, oh, that happened, and I rose. I did get knocked down flat in front of the whole world, and I rose. I didn't run away—I rose right where I'd been knocked down.
—Maya Angelou

Day 29: The Power of Gratitude

Scripture: Psalm 136:1-3

> Give thanks to the LORD, for he is good.
> *His love endures forever.*
> Give thanks to the God of gods.
> *His love endures forever.*
> Give thanks to the Lord of lords:
> *His love endures forever.*

When we are feeling down and out, it is amazing how our focus can change when we show gratitude to God and count our blessings. We know friends who keep an ongoing gratitude list to start and end their day. It is a discipline that they have started to combat loneliness, depression, or wishing for a change in their personal situation.

Research continues to prove that those individuals who regularly express gratitude have improved mental well-being, less stress, better sleep, and a boost in overall mental and physical health. Gratitude is not just good for the soul, but it does the body good. When it is hard to find our own words of thanksgiving, the Bible is a great place to turn. The amazing thing about Scripture is that it is filled with many passages in both the Old and New Testament that we can read and even pray to express gratitude.

Gratitude is simply saying thank you to God. We can show our gratitude by speaking it, through worship, and by giving back our time, talents, and treasure. When we are consumed with gratitude, we quickly forget about those things we think we are lacking. We stop comparing ourselves to others. Our gratitude toward God is thanking God for providing enough even for today. We love the various renditions of the Doxology sung in churches, both the traditional song and the contemporary version. First written by the Anglican bishop Thomas Ken (1637–1711), it is still sung in thousands of churches, denominations, and languages every single week:

> Praise God from whom all blessings flow;
> Praise him all creatures here below;
> Praise him above, ye heav'nly host;
> Praise Father, Son, and Holy Ghost.

This song is often sung in worship as the financial offering is presented to God and carried to the altar. We give from a posture of gratitude, knowing everything we have comes from God. Gratitude helps us be more generous, saves us money by cultivating contentment, and is good for our health. One more thing to be grateful for!

Reflection Questions

What are five things you are grateful for today?

How do you show gratitude to God?

What is one way you can show gratitude to God on a daily basis?

....

*Gracious God, Giver of life, help me to be a grateful person
for who you are and what you have done in my life and in the
lives of others. Let me not take anything or anyone, especially
you, for granted because all good and perfect gifts come from
you. I repent for the times I've been selfish and self-centered.
When those thoughts creep in, help me to overcome them with
gratitude. In Jesus' name, Amen.*

*Gratitude turns what we have into enough, and more.
It turns denial into acceptance, chaos into order, confusion into clarity.
. . . It makes sense of our past, brings peace for today,
and creates a vision for tomorrow.*
—Melody Beattie

Day 30: Embracing Divine Surrender

Scripture: Luke 22:42

"Father, if you are willing, take this cup from me; yet not my will, but yours be done."

surrender." Those words mean the fighting is done. In military terms, it means the other army has won. But what happens when you stop fighting the One who loves you unconditionally? When you surrender to the One who knows what you need better than you do?

In one of Jesus' final acts before his arrest, and knowing the suffering he would have to go through, Jesus prayed a prayer of surrender. Jesus lived a life of surrender and left us with the example of praying a short breath prayer when the flesh and spirit conflict with one another. Jesus did not pray a long prayer in his moment of weakness. Instead, it was short, simple, and memorable enough that Jesus' followers around the world still pray it today. Above any financial study, plan, best practices, or research, the most important thing you and I can do to better manage our money and possessions is pray the prayer that Jesus did, "Lord, not my will, but yours be done."

Surrender in our culture has a negative connotation. It could even infer weakness. It was, and yet, in Jesus' weakness, we see the demonstration of God's power displayed in both the crucifixion and the resurrection. In the recovery community, surrender is the moment where we claim we are powerless over those forces that have held us captive in our lives, like drugs and alcohol; however, that extends to materialism and our attitude regarding money. Surrender is when we begin to live our lives. We surrender to the lordship of Jesus Christ.

117

Reflection Questions

What areas in your life, financial and others, have you yet to surrender to Jesus?

What are you desperately holding on to that you have given to God but have then taken back from God?

What is a simple prayer you can use daily to remind yourself to surrender to Jesus? Write out your prayer here to God.

....

Lord Jesus, I want to give you my whole self; I not only want you to be savior of my life, saving me from my sins, but also Lord over everything I am and everything I have, because it all belongs to you. I surrender. Not my will, but yours be done. Amen.

Let God have your life; He can do more with it than you can.
—Dwight L. Moody

Pause and Reflect

As you look back at the past six days, what are you noticing?

Anything you want to confess or surrender to the Lord?

As you move forward on the journey, what is your hope or prayer?

The End of the Journey

Congratulations! You reached the end of your five-week financial journey with the Lord. How do you feel? Have you had some breakthroughs? Do you feel that you've come a long way or that there is a long way to go?

In Disney's *Homeward Bound: The Incredible Journey,* two dogs and a cat set out on a journey to return to their home. The golden retriever, Shadow, tells the other two, "Home is just over that mountain," but as they reach the top, they realize there are many more mountains and valleys ahead.

The truth is we will forever be on a journey with the Lord until we reach our eternal home in heaven, where we have an inheritance that is greater than any earthly fortune. In the meantime, we will have many journeys and destinations along the way. We can get overwhelmed by what is ahead, or we can pause at the top of this mountain, this destination we have just reached, and enjoy the view. We can stop to notice all that we have done and give God thanks.

Take a moment now. Look back at the "Pause and Reflect" section at the end of each week. What do you notice? Any big themes or patterns?

As we have seen, gratitude is a powerful tool. Take a moment to give God thanks for anything on your heart after the past five weeks.

Take a moment to write out your own closing prayer, surrendering everything to God again and asking God for help where you need the Lord to move.

We leave you with this closing benediction. Receive this as a blessing in your life:

As you go forth from this journey, may you know the awesome love of God our Father, the grace of our Lord Jesus Christ, and the power and presence of the Holy Spirit in all areas of your life. You are blessed to be a blessing. Amen.

SCAN HERE to learn more about Invite Press, a premier publishing imprint created to invite people to a deeper faith and living relationship with Jesus Christ.